Carving a Kid's Size
ROCKING HORSE

Text written with
and photography by
Douglas Congdon-Martin

D1514716

Tom
Wolfe

Schiffer
Publishing Ltd

77 Lower Valley Road, Atglen, PA 19310

CONTENTS

Printed in China

ISBN: 0-88740-852-4

Library of Congress Cataloging-in-Publication Data

Wolfe, Tom (Tom James)
        Carving a kid's size rocking horse/ Tom Wolfe; text written with and photography by Douglas Congdon-Martin.
        p.   cm.
        ISBN 0-88740-852-4 (pbk.)
        1. Wooden toy making. 2. Wood-carving.
3. Rocking horses in art. I. Congdon-Martin, Dou-glas. II. Title.
TT174.5.W6W637 1995
745.592--dc20   95-30183
                                                      CIP

Published by Schiffer Publishing, Ltd.
77 Lower Valley Road
Atglen, PA 19310
Please write for a free catalog.
This book may be purchased from the publisher.
Please include $2.95 postage.
Try your bookstore first.

We are interested in hearing from authors
with book ideas on related subjects.

INTRODUCTION

I recently became a grandfather for the first time. It's a nice feeling and a pretty good deal. I get all the fun without any of the responsibility!

Most grandparents have great big dreams for their grandchildren, and they help them along by giving them special gifts. If they want the kid to be a football player they give them a helmet and a ball. If they want her to be a doctor they give her a toy medical kit. Well, I'd like my grandson to be a woodcarver, but Nancy wouldn't let me give him a carving knife! I guess I'll have to wait until his first birthday.

In the meantime, he'll have to settle for this rocking horse. It was a big project, but it was fun. It the kind of thing that will be used and enjoyed now, and then passed on to the next generation and the one after that. I can just hear the stories..."your great-great-grandpa carved this with his own hands."

If you have that same kind of dream of immortality, select some real nice wood and pay particular attention to the construction of the horse. If you are careful with this, the horse you carve should have years loving, joyful service. Enjoy!

CARVING THE ROCKING HORSE

THE WOOD YOU WILL NEED

The project I carved here used basswood boards, but other woods could be used as well. You could even use standard 3/4 shelving from the lumber yard, though the horse would be a little skinnier than the one we have built.

You will need:
7 boards: 96" x 1" x 7"
2 boards: 72" x 1" x 7"

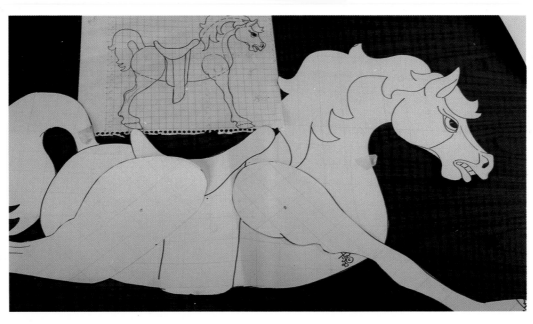

The pattern in the book is 1/3 the size of the actual rocking horse. Unfortunately the limitations of publishing make it necessary to cut it in pieces. Copy the pieces and paste it back together. The numbered grid should make this easy. It also allows you to enlarge it to a grid of 1 1/2" squares. When you have enlarged the pattern to full size, cut out the pieces from poster board stock. The dotted line on the shoulders define the outermost layer of the body.

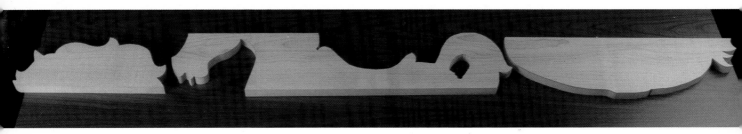

The pieces of the horse are built up of several boards. I am using stock that is 7" wide by 1" thick. You can just as easily use 3/4" stock, making your horse just a little bit thinner. The body is basically seven layers thick, with the grains of alternating layers going in opposite directions for strength. The center layer and two others are cut with the grain going from the top to the bottom. Each of these three layers can be cut from one eight foot board.

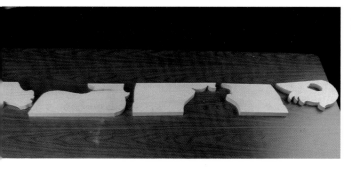

The layer on either side of the center has the grain going from head to tail. Each of these two layers can be cut from a board 7" by 8 feet.

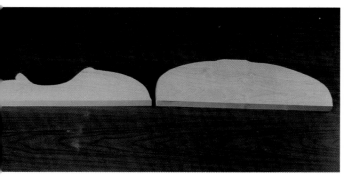

The outside layers have grain running from head to tail, but the head and tail are missing to save carving. You need two sets of these, one for each side.

Each leg is three layers thick, so you will need to cut 6 hind leg pieces and 6 foreleg pieces. The grain runs the length of the leg.

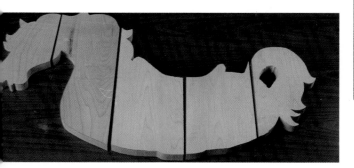

Assemble and glue each layer, before gluing one layer to another.

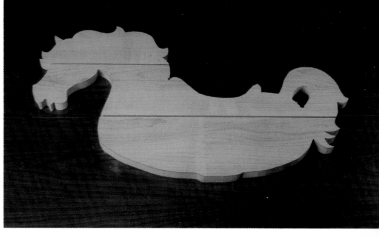

Glue along the edges, keeping the glue from beading on the sides. Any excess glue will need to be scraped before joining the layers.

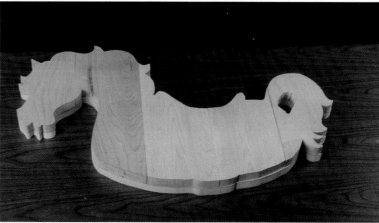

The outside layer has only two pieces.

When the layers are dried, clean away the excess glue and glue one layer to the other. The center layer has the grain running from top to bottom. Move out from there with the grain of each layer going the opposite direction of the one below. A skinnier horse, like the painted one shown in the gallery, can be built with five layers. In that case, the grain of center layer goes from head to tail.

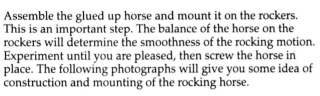

Assemble the glued up horse and mount it on the rockers.
This is an important step. The balance of the horse on the
rockers will determine the smoothness of the rocking motion.
Experiment until you are pleased, then screw the horse in
place. The following photographs will give you some idea of
construction and mounting of the rocking horse.

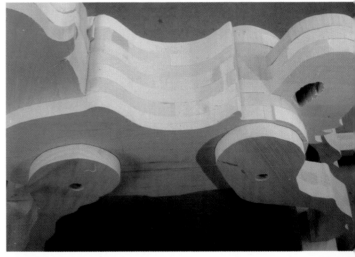

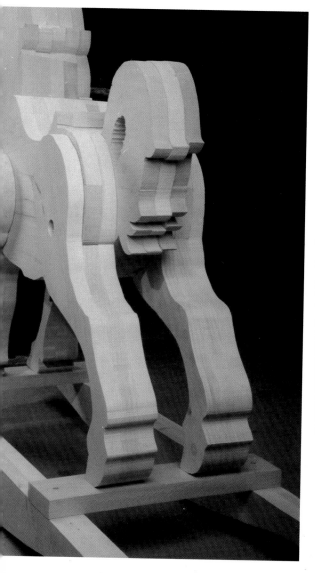

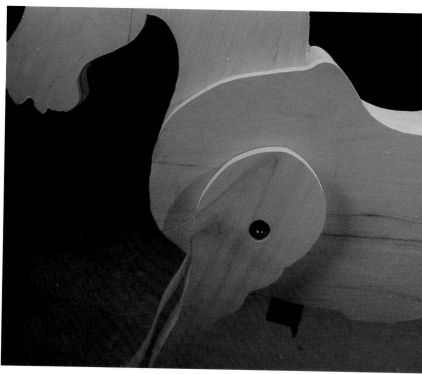

When you are satisfied, number each leg and its position on the rocker, then remove the horse from the rockers.

Mark the legs before removing them from the body to assure that they go back in the correct place, and that you carve around the joint.

The position of the eye can be set with the pattern of by drawing intersecting lines from the back of the jaw to the front of the forelock, and from the top of the upper lip to the crook at the back of the head, where the mane begins. This position is much easier to set before carving begins. Drill a hole 1" in diameter. I use a Forstner drill.

A 1" recessing hole where the bolts come through the legs, allows me to use a 1" dowel to fill them in.

Threaded 1/4" rods hold the legs. They should go all the way through the hip and shoulder. You should drill this on a drill press so the hole is nice and straight.

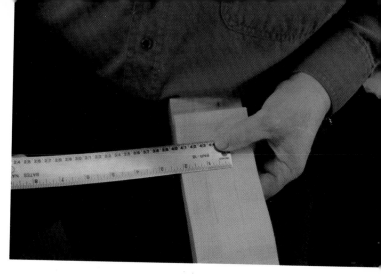

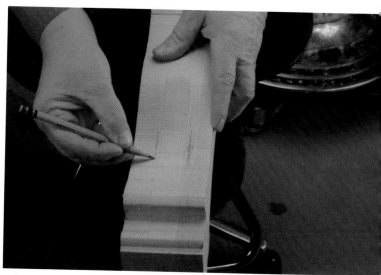

Center your ruler on the front of the leg and mark the width.

With the legs and rockers removed, I mount the piece on a carving hold down. Mine is made from the base of an old dentist's chair. This allows me to move it up and down, and adjust it to any angle. Any hold down will do, but I strongly suggest a ball joint.

Hold your pencil so it acts as a depth gauge and extend this line.

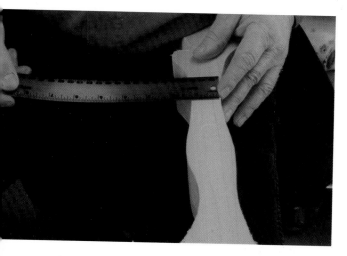

To transfer the widths of the leg to the front and back surfaces, I begin by measuring at the side of the ankle. It is 1 1/8" thick.

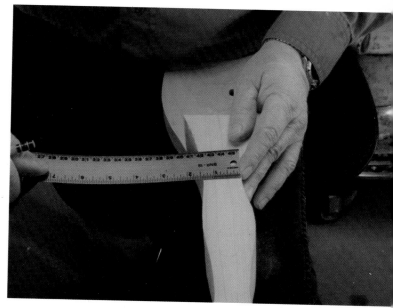

Above the knee the leg thickness narrows to 1 3/8".

Transfer this measurement to the front, centering your ruler.

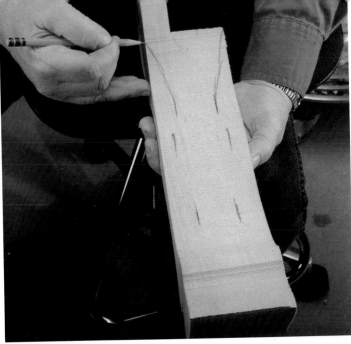

Extend the lines.

When these three dimensions are transferred to the front extend the lines to the top of the leg...

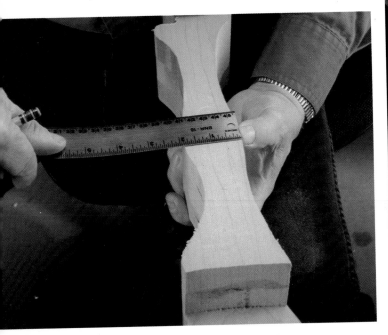

The knee measures 1 7/8". Follow the same procedure.

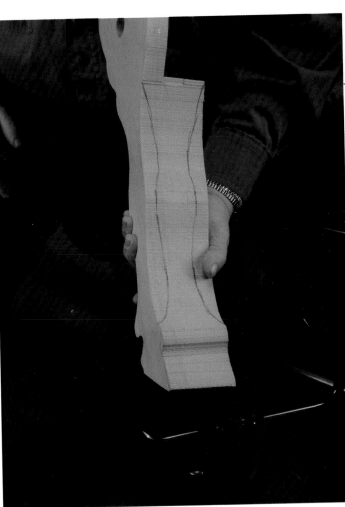

and to the hoof to establish the correct shape.

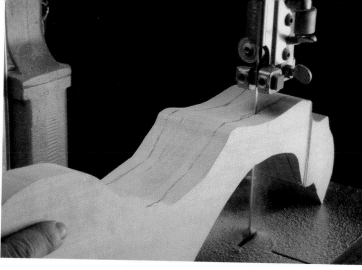

Do the same on the back legs. The measurement above the knee is 2".

Cut the shapes of the legs on the band saw.

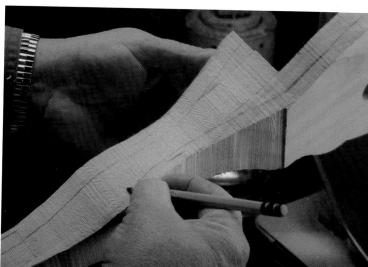

Above the ankle it is about 1 3/8".

With the basic shape set we can also knock of the corners on the band saw. In preparation this, mark a line about 1/2" in from the corners. This will give you a guide so you don't overcut.

At the knee it is 2 1/4". That said, you should remember that this is a sculptured item. Trust your eye as much as your ruler to make it look right.

Tilt the band saw table to 45 degrees and cut off the edges.

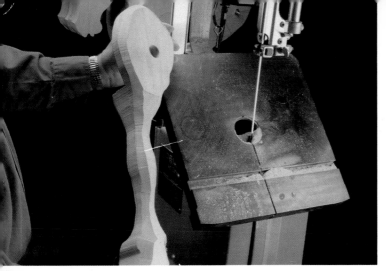

The result.

Mark the back of the saddle so you don't take too much away.

Mark the area where the stirrup piece will go on the saddle. It should be about 3 1/2" up from the belly at the bulge for the saddle.

Cut down the edge of the shoulder. This is an area you know will be rounded off, so you can be pretty aggressive.

Draw the square shape of the stirrup piece.

Continue on the chest in the same way.

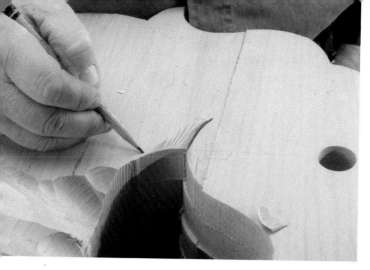

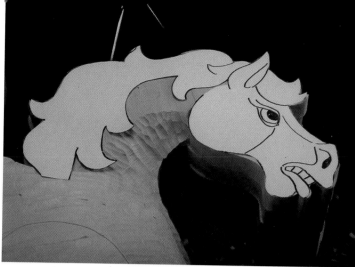

The neck can be done too, but before going too far be sure to draw in the jaw line so you don't cut it away by mistake.

Copy the head and mane pattern and cut around them. Lay it on the head and trace around it.

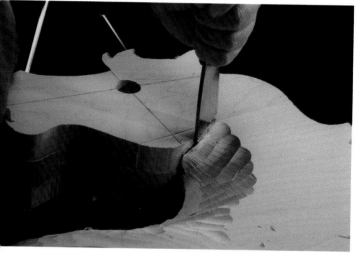

At the jaw, cut a stop in the line...

Outline the mane with a v-tool.

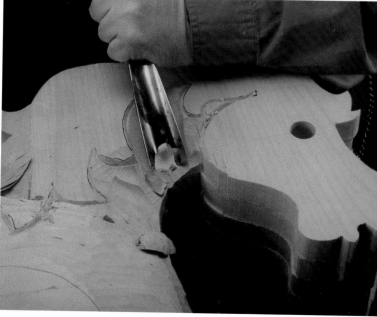

and trim back to it from the neck. This will leave you a nice clean jaw line.

Clean the neck between the locks of the mane.

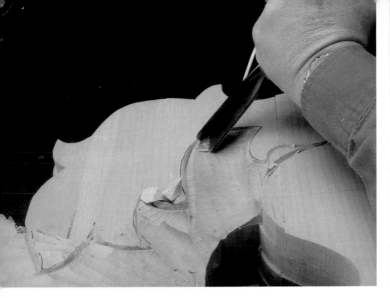

Deepen the line...

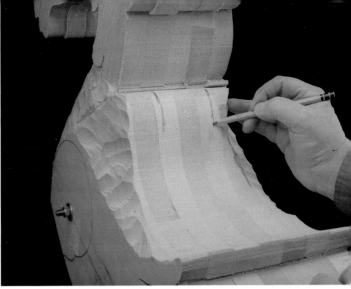

Before going too far, mark the horn of the saddle, about 2 1/2" wide.

and clean up the surface with a gouge.

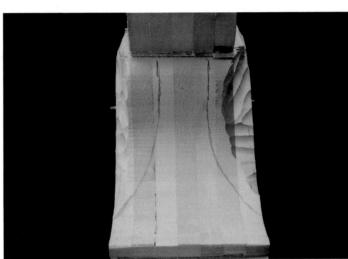

Continue with the line of the seat, flaring it out as it moves toward the back.

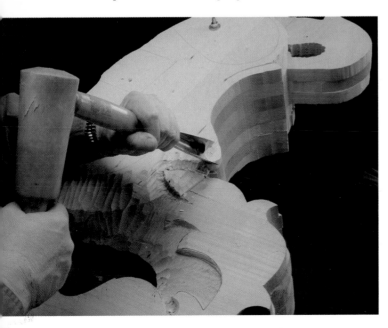

Begin to round off the saddle.

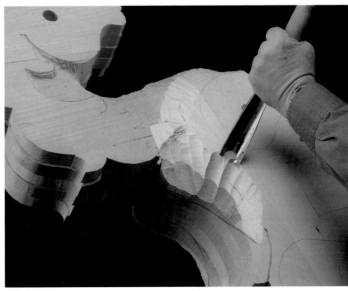

Shape the sides of the saddle back to the line.

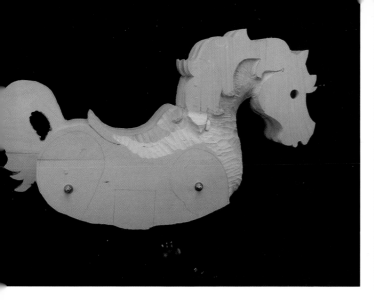

Progress.

Find a gouge that fits the curve of the ear line, and drive it in to make a stop.

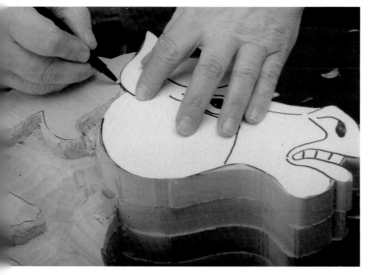

Cut the pattern so you can draw the back of the ear.

Follow the stop line with a skew to deepen it.

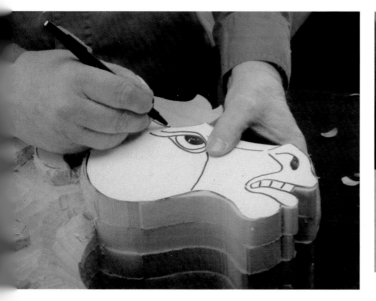

Cut it again to allow you to draw the front of the ear and the bottom edge of the forelock.

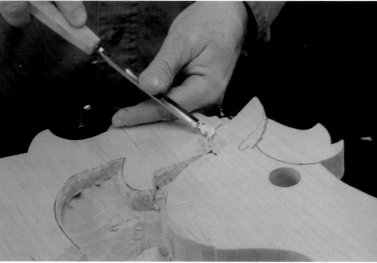

Cut back to the stop from the mane and the forelock. Deepen the stop and repeat the process until you get to the proper depth.

Mark the gap between the ears. It is about 2" wide.

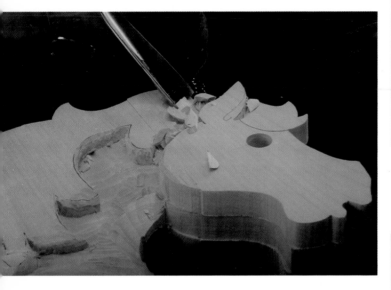

When the lines are set, you can switch to a larger gouge for removing larger amounts of wood.

Cut away the top edge of the mane.

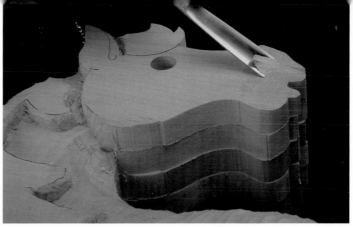

Reduce the width of the face, starting at the nose.

With this project you may wish to use a power tool like this for some of the rough removal. The trouble with these tools is that you can overdo it in a skinny minute.

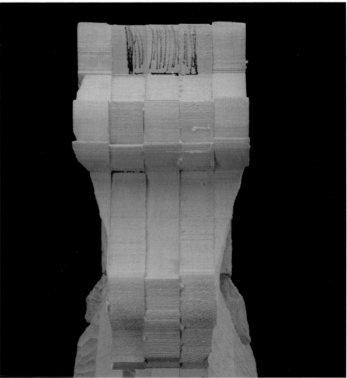

At the end of the nose I have reduced it to three inches. This tapers out to about 4 inches at the eyes. The ears are a full 5 inches.

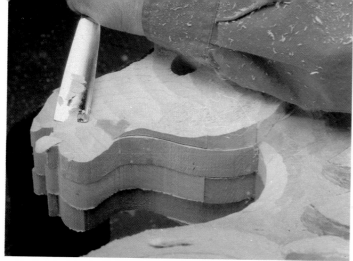

Even with the power tool, you will need to go back with a chisel and clean it up.

Cut a stop on the front of the ear at an angle.

Saw the lines of the gap between the ears.

Cut back to it from the forelock.

Chisel out the gap. The saw cuts act as stops to protect the ears.

Mark the bottom edge of the forelock.

Cut a stop in the line with a gouge that follows its curve.

Come in at the base of the ear to bring out the bulbous part of the ear where it meets the jaw.

With a smaller flat gouge, cut back to the stop. Go easy at first so you don't bust an edge off.

Deepen the stop...

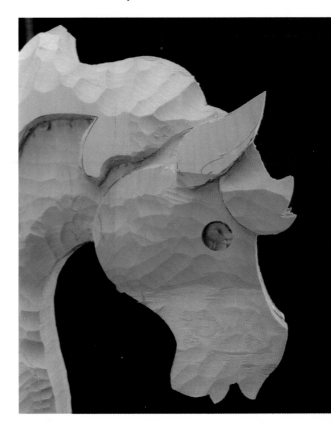

Progress on the head.

and come back to it again. This time I can use a little bigger tool and be a little more aggressive.

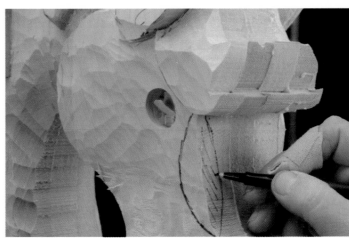

Mark the top edge of the muzzle to be removed. This cut will come in about 3/4" on the top and 1" on the side.

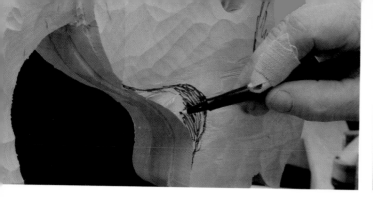

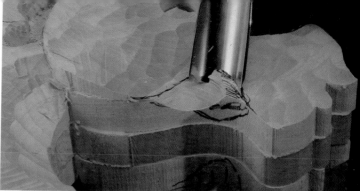

Do the same on the bottom edge, coming about 1" on the underside, and up about 1 1/4" on the side.

Do the same on the underside of the muzzle.

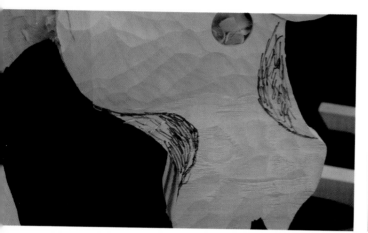

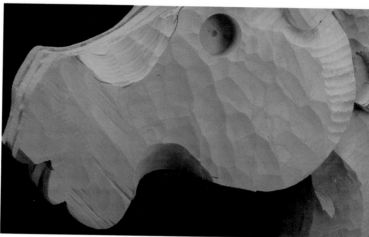

The areas to be removed are darkened.

The result from the side...

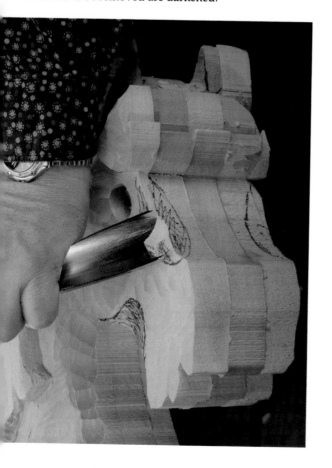

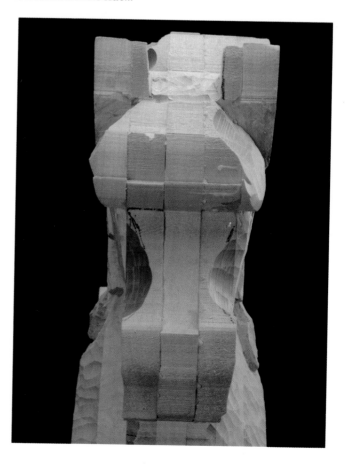

Cut away the darkened area with a gouge.

and straight on.

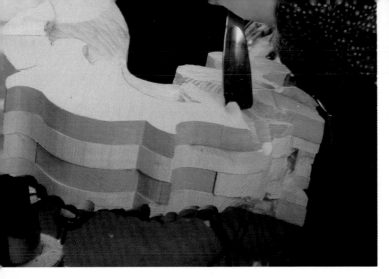

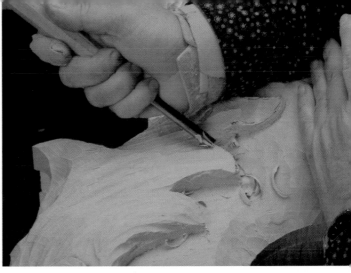

Continue rounding over the top edge of the mane.

Use the smaller gouge to soften the edges of the mane's locks...

When I get to the end of the mane, I switch to a narrower gouge and begin to follow the line of the hair. That piece sticking up will have to be rounded over or removed to provide for child safety.

and add some major hair lines.

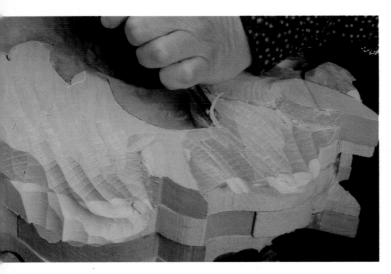

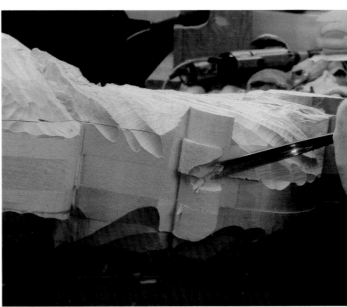

As you move closer to the head, switch to a smaller gouge. The lines you leave will become part of the design.

This lower flare of the mane needs to be softened and defined. I begin by creating a gap in the center.

Shape from the outside in, and soften the point of the hook.

I've decided to reduce the right hand flare to a swirl. You may decide to leave it, but whichever you decide, carve it so it won't harm the rider.

Cut a stop at the line where the flare meets the mane...

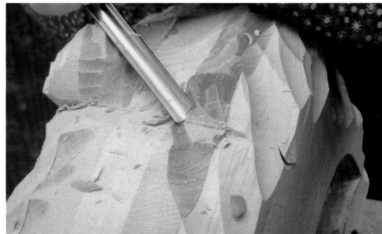

Add hair lines over the top of the mane so the flow naturally.

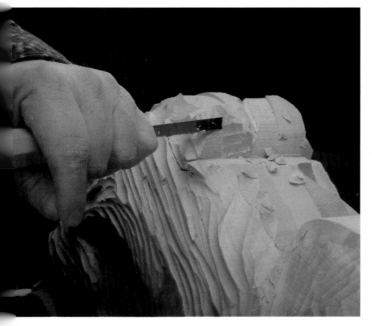

and shape the flare back to it.

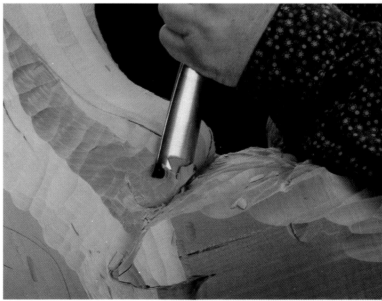

Before going too far I need to round over the horn of the saddle.

Use a gouge to define the profile shape of the horn.

A power burr will reduce the sides of the saddle horn very nicely.

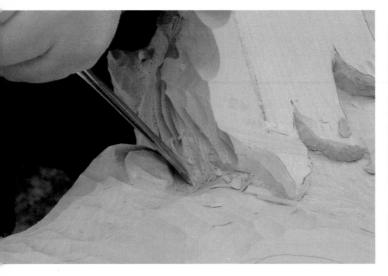

When the basic shape is established you want to deepen the separation between the mane and the horn. Cut a stop in the line of the horn...

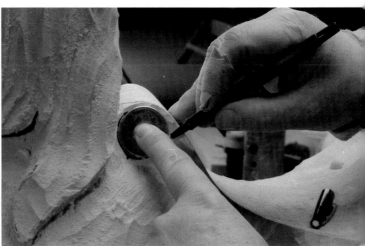

When the surface of the horn is prepared, and fairly flat, use a coin or other round object to draw its outline, three-quarters of the way around.

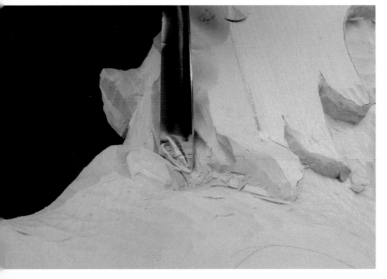

and come back to it from the mane. Repeat the process on the other side, making it match.

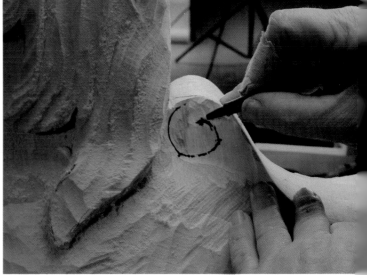

Remove the coin and finish the design in a spiral.

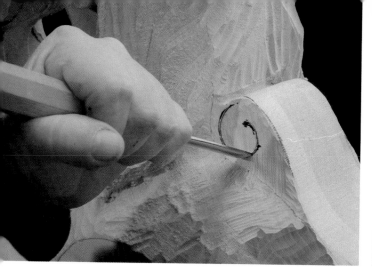

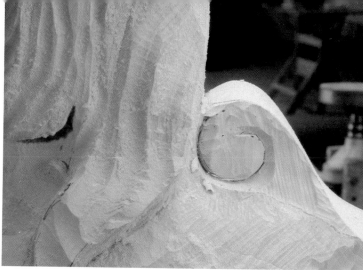

Into the line drive a chisel that matches the curve of the spiral to create a stop.

Round over the top edge of the horn for this result.

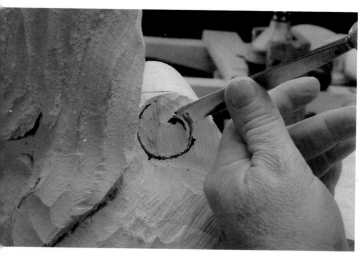

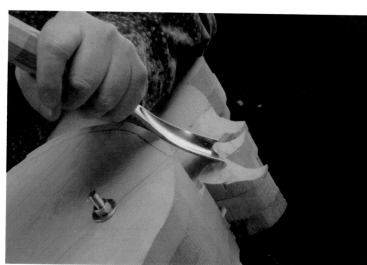

Cut back to the stop with the same chisel.

Round over edges of the tail.

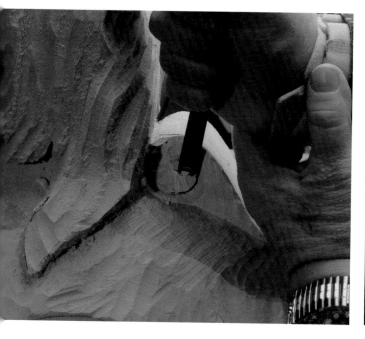

Clean up the surface of the spiral.

The result. Do the same trimming on the other side.

The boards that make up the hip do not always come out even. To fix it we can use a chisel...

Where the tail returns to the hip, cut a deep stop. The tail will roll back to it. You want it to look like the tail is not attached, even though, for strength, it has to be.

or a power tool. Try not to go beyond the line you drew for the leg, though if you must, the leg can be adjusted slightly later.

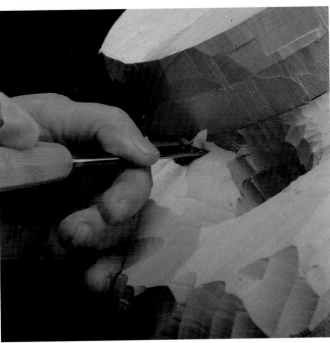

Cut back to the stop from the tail.

Carry the line of the hip through the opening in the tail.

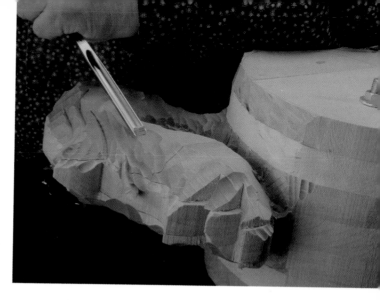

Next I will add some of the major hair movement lines using a #9 half-round gouge.

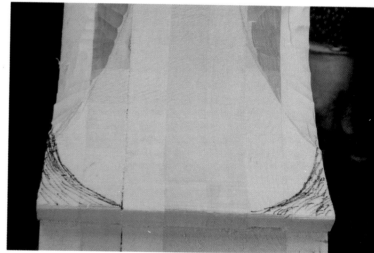

Mark the area around the back of the saddle to be removed. This will be cut straight down.

Progress on the tail.

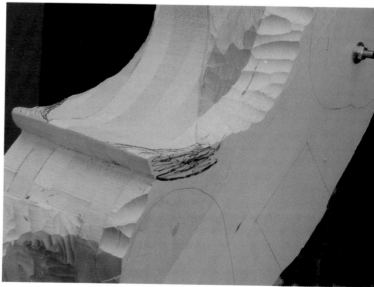

Mark the side too. This will be round over from the hip.

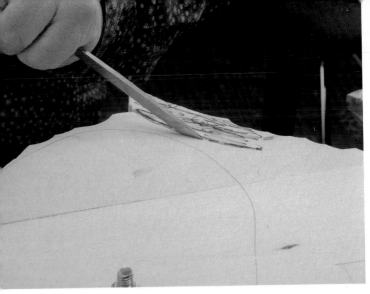

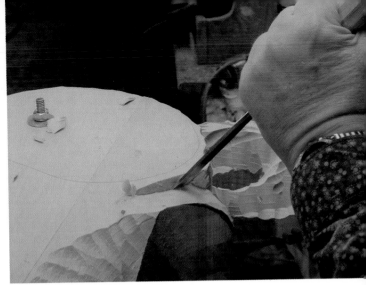

Cut a stop in the side line. I am using a skew which chases pretty good on a straight run like this.

Reset the stop...

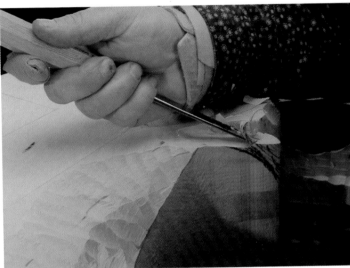

Go down the middle to lift off a nice smooth piece.

before rounding the hip over to the saddle.

This creates a nice edge on the hip, so I can trim the back of the saddle without damaging the surrounding area.

Undercut the saddle a little bit more to give it more depth. Repeat on the other side.

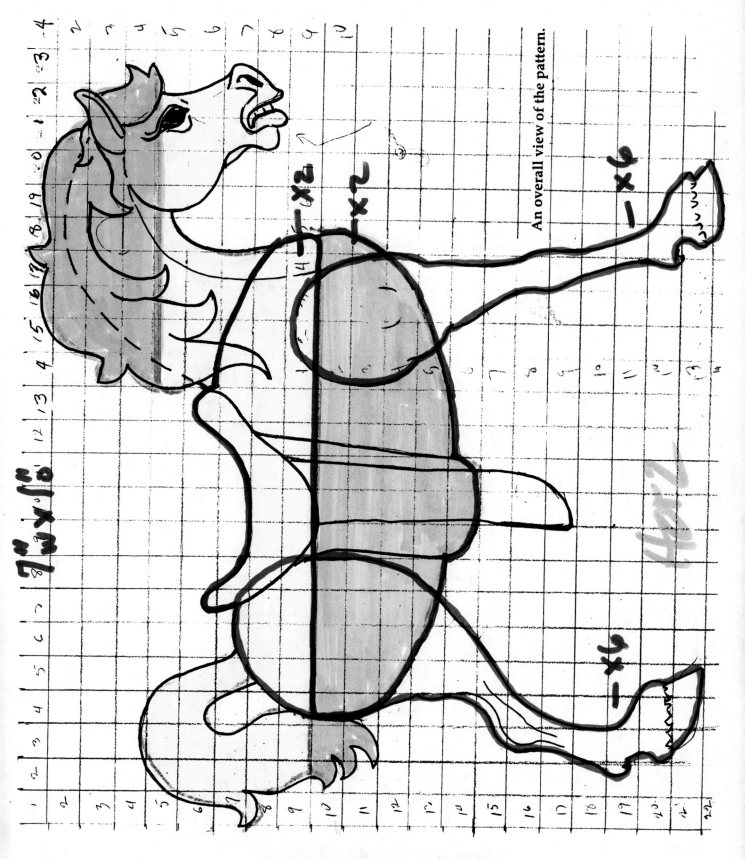

An overall view of the pattern.

PATTERNS

PATTERNS

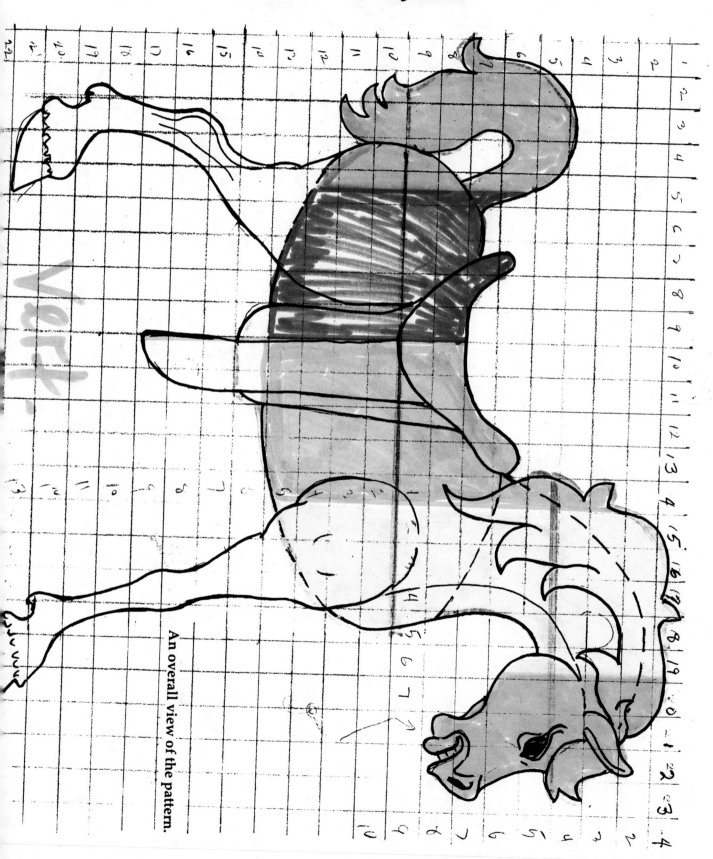

An overall view of the pattern.

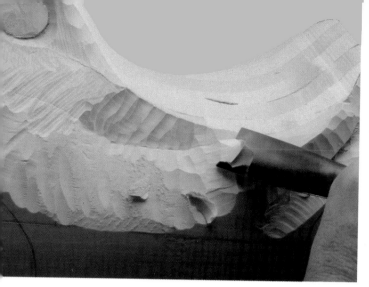

Round the top of the saddle carrying the line of the back lip down the side.

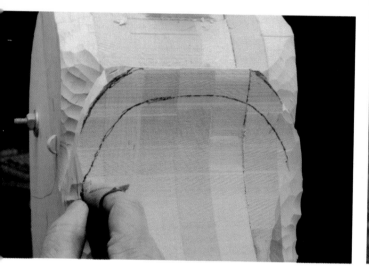

You want to leave a thick (1") rim around the back of the saddle for strength.

The result.

I am using a ball-shaped cutting burr to shape the rim of the saddle around the seat area.

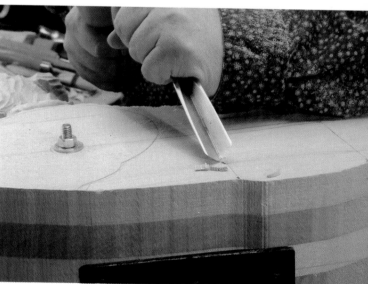

Cut around the stirrup piece outline with a v-tool, keeping the guiding edge pretty much vertical.

A straight chisel cleans up the line and makes it straighter.

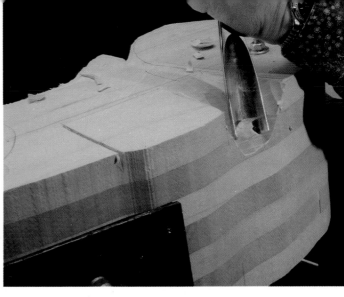

Carry the cut around the belly about two layers (2" in this case).

Go around the leg lines with a u-gouge. In this spot you don't want a sharp line.

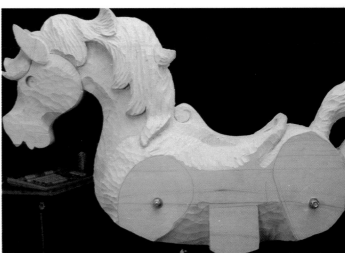

Progress.

Knock off the corner of the belly at a 45 degree angle.

Time for details. Begin by outline the shape of the ears from the front...

and back.

As I worked on the mane flair, I decided that the smaller left hand lock would be removed.

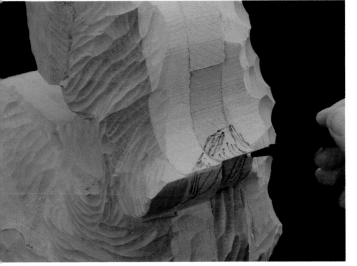

I also want to mark the shape of the upper flare in the mane. I'm going to have a lock flying out to the right, and a smaller lock on the left, with this gap in the middle.

Use the same tool to rough of the shape of the ear.

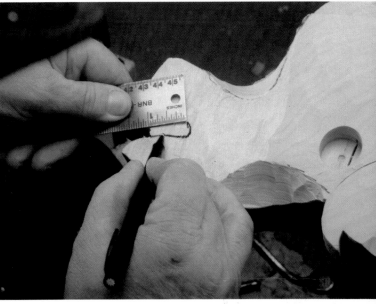

I'm using a power cutter to remove the wood, but a gouge would work as well, if slower.

Draw the area of the mouth, going back about 1"

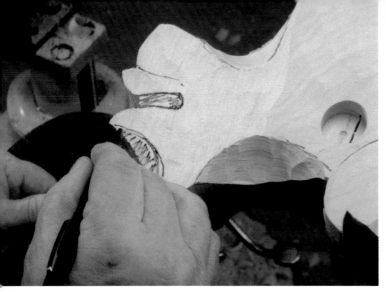

The corner at the front of the nose will be knocked off.

Round up the jaw line and the cheeks.

for this result.

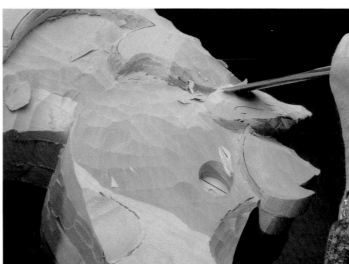

Round the back of the ear.

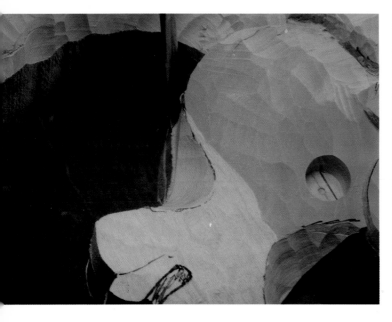

Smooth off the underside of the jaw.

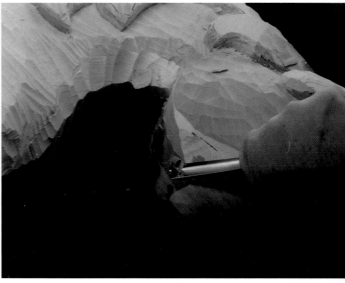

Continue rounding the forelock, and the strong edges of the face.

With a gouge, define the underside of the lip.

Do the same on the upper and lower lip lines.

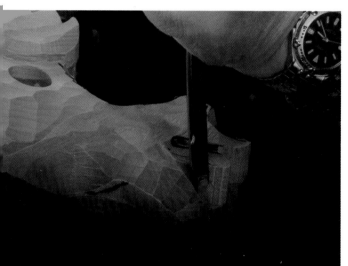

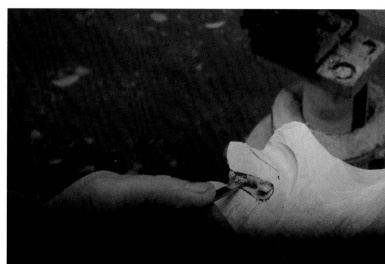

Continue around the front.

Clean the mouth area back to the level of the teeth.

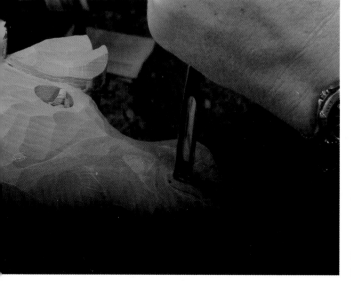

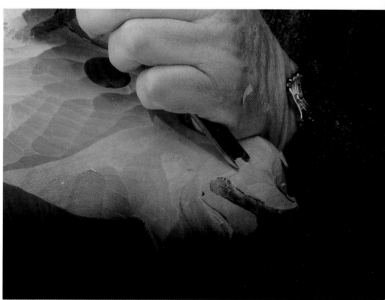

Find a gouge to fit the curve of the back of the mouth and drive it in for a stop.

Come over the top lip with a gouge to bring out the lip.

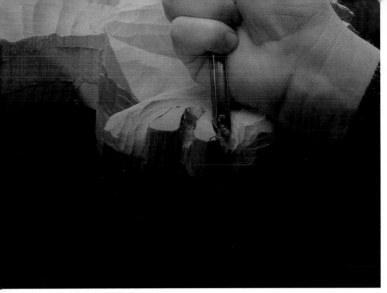

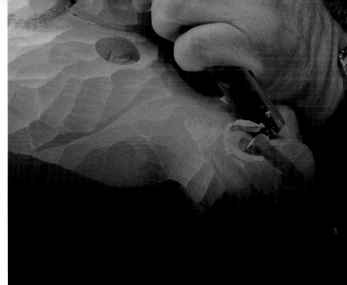

Continue around to the front of the mouth. The cut should fade out as it reaches the center of the mouth.

When the general shape is set, knock off the sharp edges of the lips.

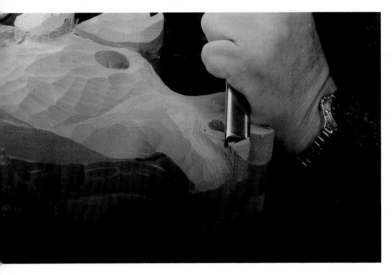

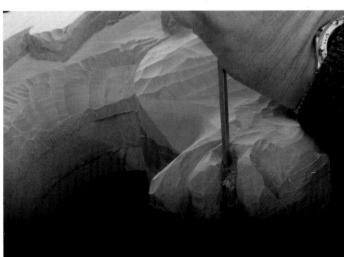

Begin rounding the lip by knocking off the corners, bottom...

I want to deepen the teeth a little more, so I cut a stop along the line where the teeth meet the lips, upper and lower...

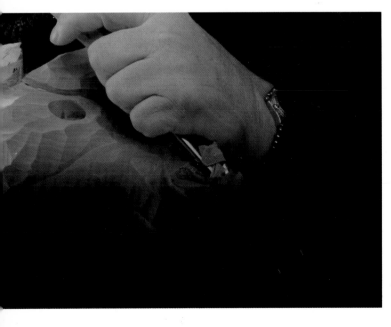

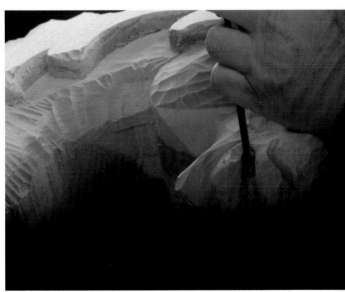

and top.

and clean out the teeth with a veiner.

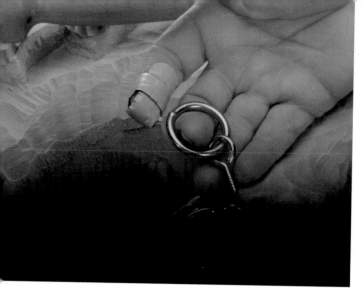

The hardware for the reins is an O-ring which I have run through an eye-screw.

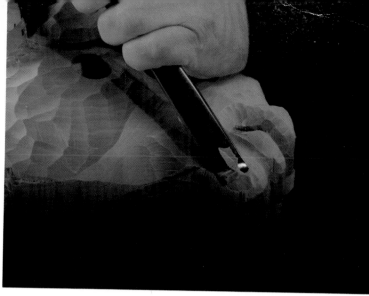

Continue to soften the lines and refine the face.

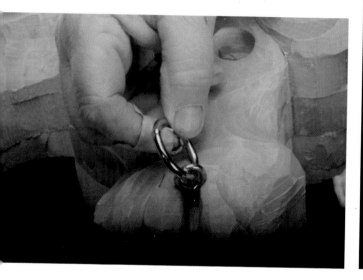

I test fit it at this point, to see how much I need to open up the back of the lips.

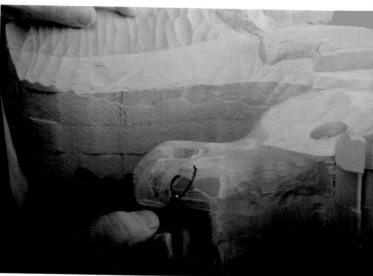

Mark the nostril. This is tentative until the other side is finished. Go ahead and carve the other side of the face in the same way.

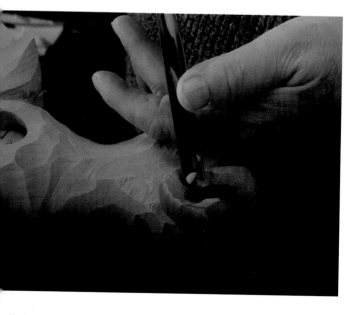

Enlarge the area for the O-ring.

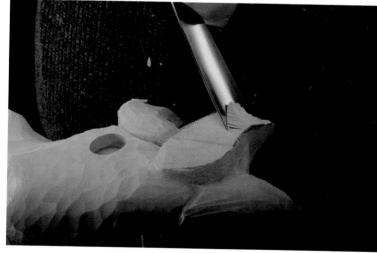

The back outside edge of the ear slopes down to about half the thickness of the ear.

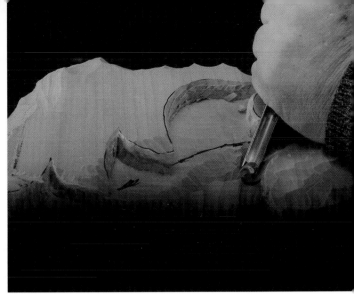

The bottom outside edge is just rounded off.

Cup down from this line to the bottom of the neck. I begin at the head with a small gouge...

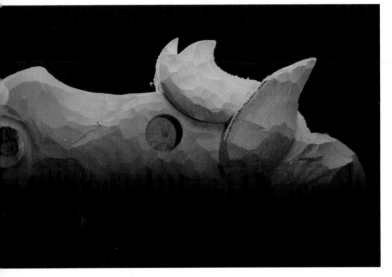

This is the result.

and continue with a larger gouge. I have uncovered a gap in the joint of the wood which I will need to fill later.

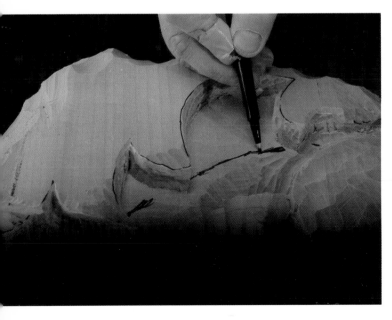

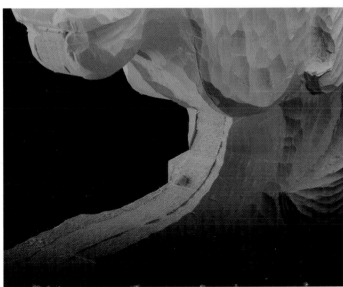

The neck muscle follows a line that goes about here.

The result.

Returning to the ear, I shape the inside of its back.

Apply glue and tap it in place.

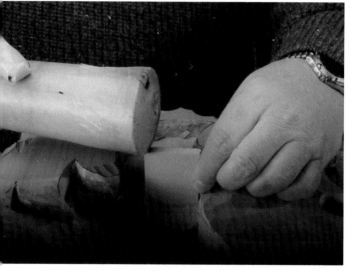

Since I am probably going to finish this natural I make a wedge to fill the gap in the neck. I drive it in a little to see about how far it will go in.

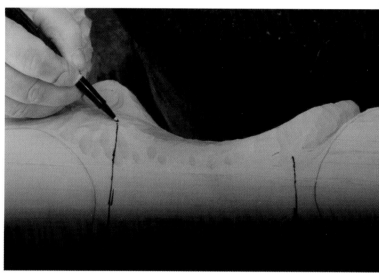

Draw the lines of the saddle.

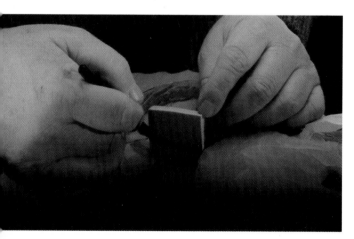

Mark the cut off line, remove the wedge, and cut it with a saw. By doing this I can do the final trim with a knife after it is glued in place. Otherwise I would need to use a chisel and would likely bust up the wedge.

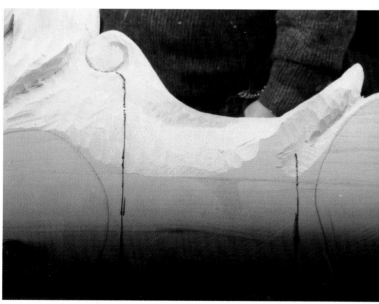

The result. Be sure to match the two sides.

With chisels that match the curves of the saddle, cut a stop around its outline.

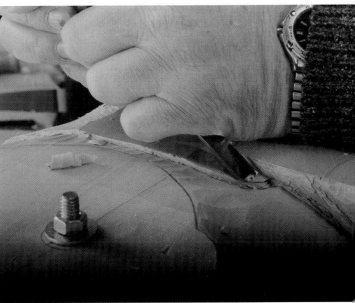

Clean up your marks.

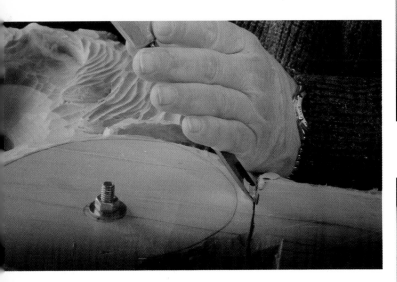

Cut back to the stop from the body of the horse, first with short, easy strokes to set the line...

Now that the patch is dry on the neck we can shave it off.

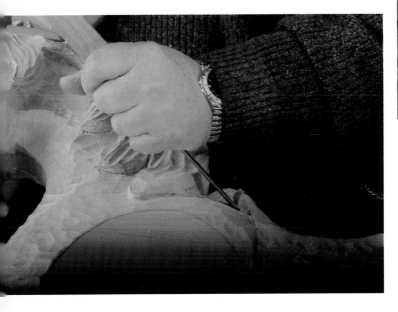

then with longer strokes to blend the body back to the saddle.

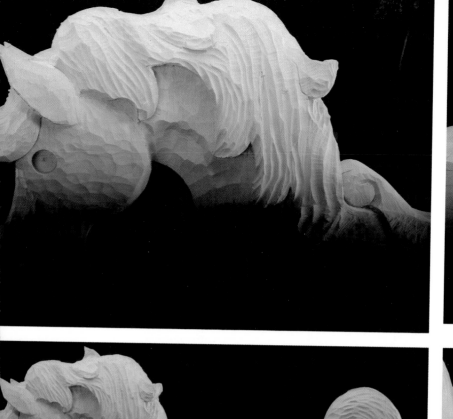

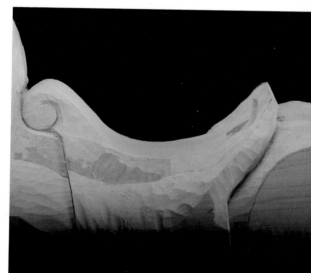

Ready for detailing.

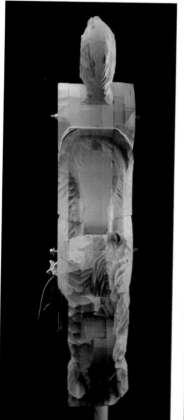

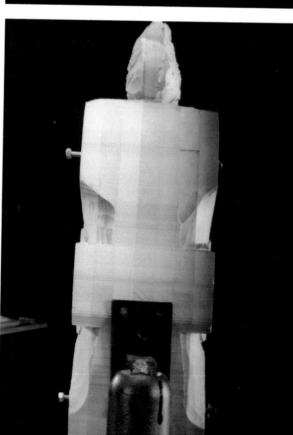

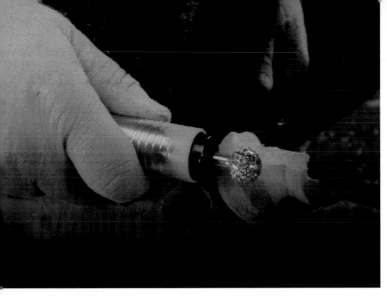

This ball used on a flexible shaft tool will contour and texture the hair of the mane, at the same time.

The same tool hollows the front of the ears.

Follow the flow of the hair with the tool, leaving the lines of the hair as you go.

Continue down the back of the mane. You have the possibility of creating some dramatic hair flow here. I am considering a cut through on this upper lock.

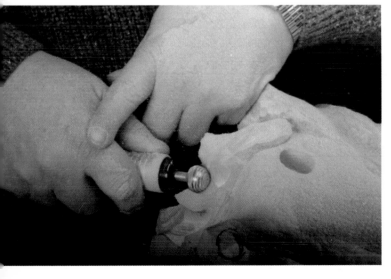

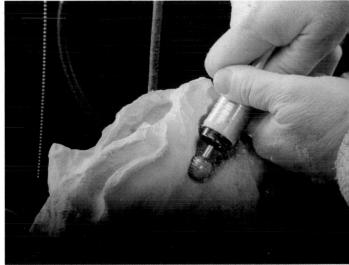

You can use this to create the different locks of hair as well, by gouging the space between them.

You can create deep folds with the grinder...

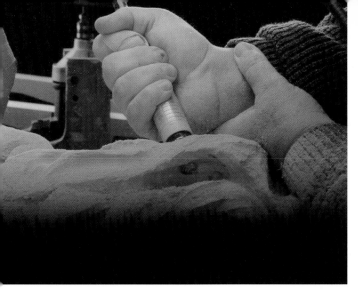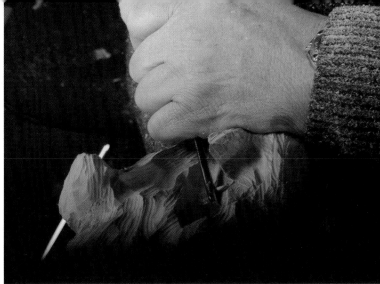

and add cut-throughs in one or two places. This increases the drama of the mane a lot.

As nice as cut-throughs are to look at, they are fragile. The one I was working on broke, so I'm going to have to redesign a little. The other seems stronger.

Progress on one side.

I'll remove the lower part all together.

I'm going back with a v-tool to sharpen up some of the rounded edges left by the power tool.

With the veiner I add definition to some of the lines of the mane.

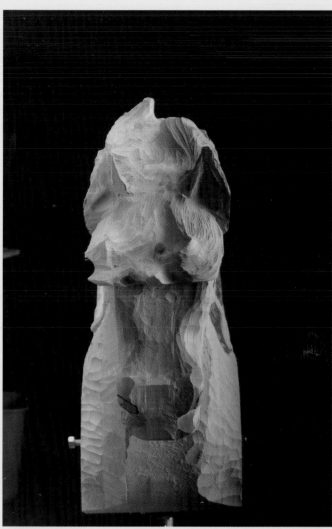

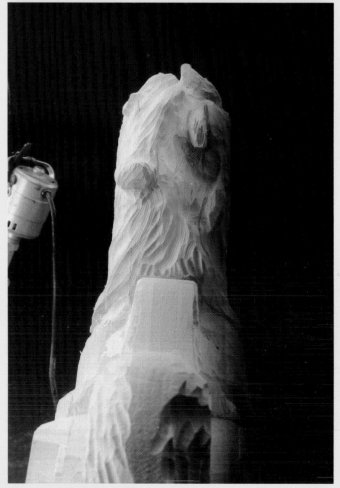

Progress on the mane.

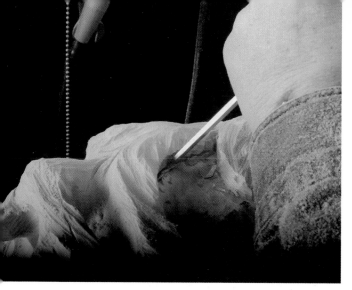

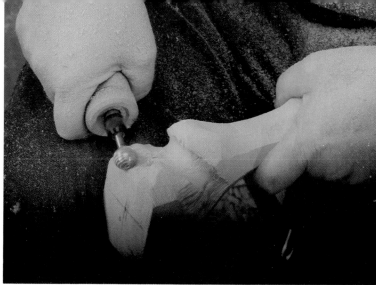

Redefine and sharpen the edges of the mane as needed.

Carve out the frog at the back of the hoof.

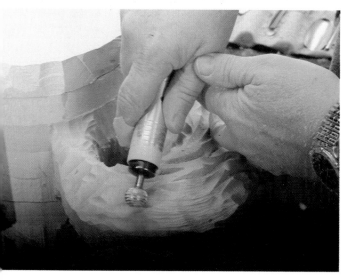

Finish the tail in the same way.

Carry the line of the hock around to the front, blending it there with the lower leg.

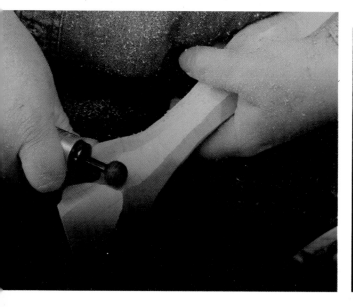

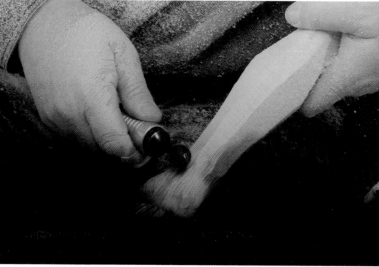

Moving to the leg, we begin by bringing the line under the hock around to the sides.

Carve another indentation where the hair meets the hoof. This too goes all the way around the hoof.

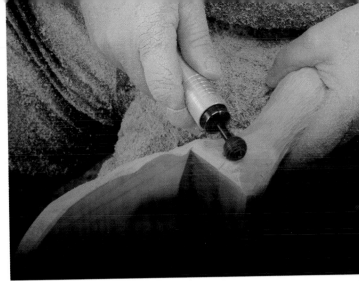

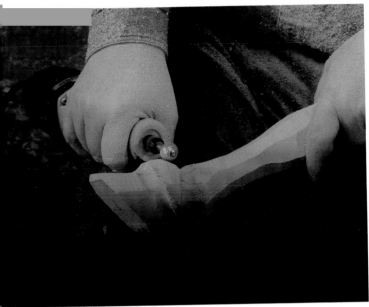

Round over the hair area.

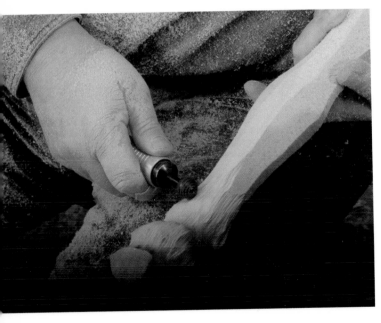

Work your way up the leg with the power grinder. Short strokes will give you the effect of hair. At the same time you round the leg from the octagonal shape you created during sawing.

I purposely stay away from the joining edge until the leg is mounted on the horse. This gives me room to blend the body and the leg.

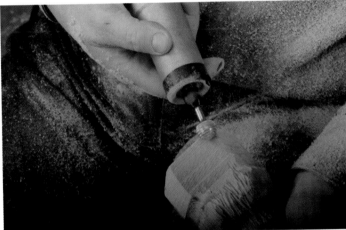

I'm going to even the hoof up with the power grinder...

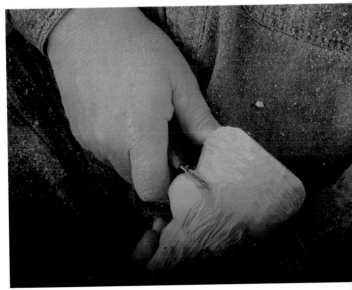

and go back and dress it up with a knife. Make a stop in the top of the hoof...

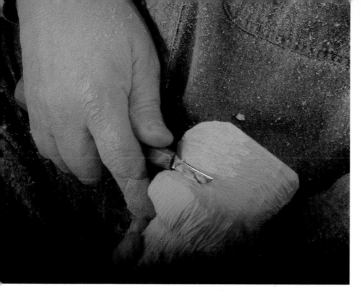

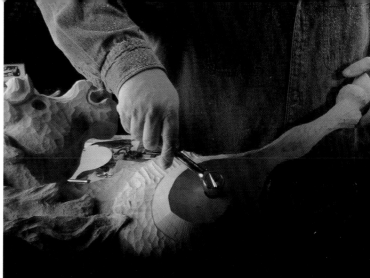

and cut back to it. For someone like me, who does almost all his carving with a knife, it seems strange that this is the first time I've touched a knife in this whole project. Suffering from "tool withdrawal" I guess.

Align the leg with the marks and tighten it in place.

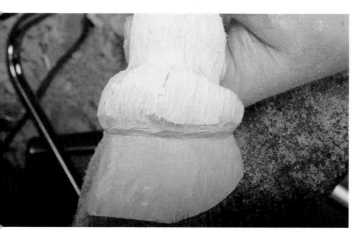

The carved hoof.

Begin by dressing up the haunch with the chisel. I want to take away the hard line of the saw and round things up.

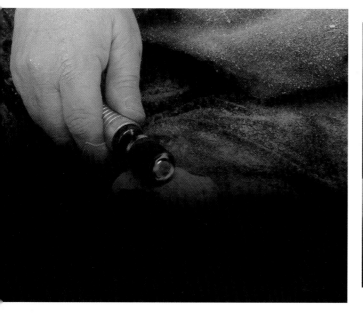

A light sanding and we're ready to fit the legs on the horse.

The result. Notice that I didn't go all the way to the edge yet. I will wait until the leg is glued in place for this last step.

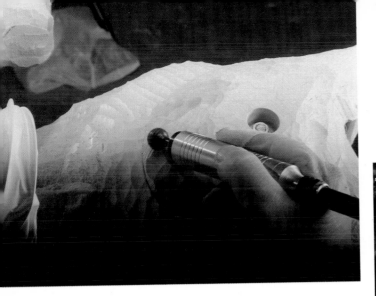

Add some hair to the haunch with the rotary tool, blending it with the hair of the lower leg.

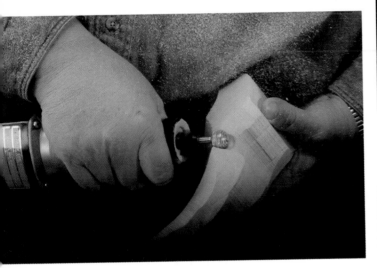

Do the back legs in the same way.

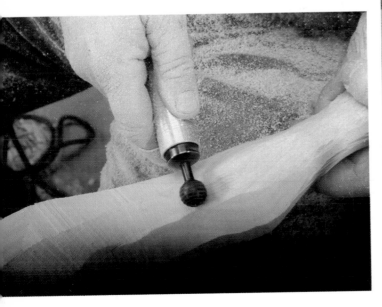

The back knee has two grooves on each side of the leg. The first is at the back of the joint, paralleling the line of the leg.

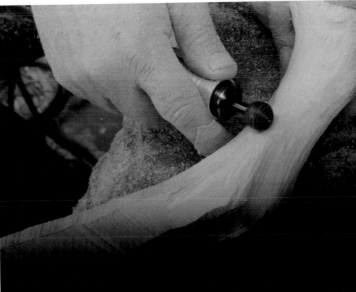

The other is on the side of the joint. Make the depression with a grinder or gouge and repeat on the other side of the joint.

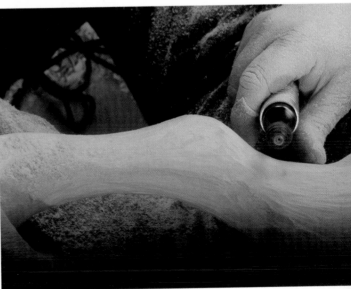

The result.

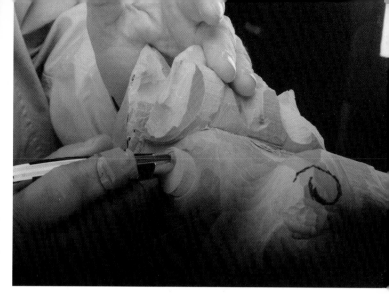

The legs in place.

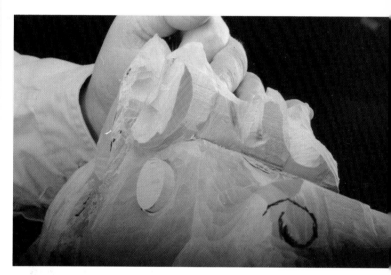

Stick a dowel in the eye hole, mark it and cut it off so it protrudes out a little from the face. Glue and tap it in place.

This little bit will be rounded over.

Before gluing, I can round the back hips. I don't go into the body with the chisel for fear of busting something off. I will use the power tool for the blending.

Remove the body from the holding device, and apply glue to the legs and body. With white carpenter's glue you have some time to make adjustments, as long as you don't clamp it.

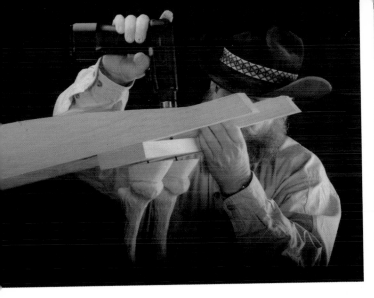

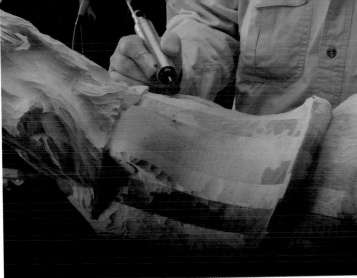

Attach the horse to the rockers. This will assure that the legs are in the proper position.

When the glue has set, remove the rockers and remount the horse on the holding jig. A ball burr on a rotary tool is used with short strokes to make hair lines on the body.

Tighten the legs in place. This will create the pressure for a good glue joint.

Blend the joint between the leg and the body.

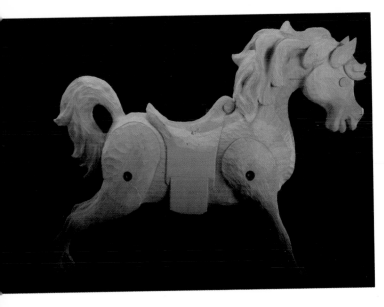

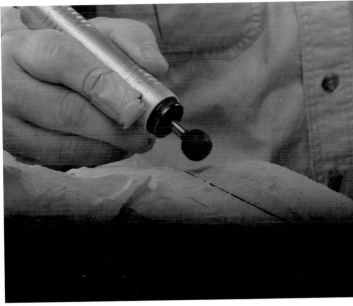

Ready for the final refinement.

Carry the hair lines from the body to the leg.

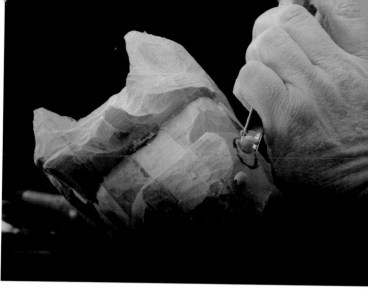

Soften any hard edges, like here in the neck. At the same time you will continue to add the hair texture.

Carve the nostrils...

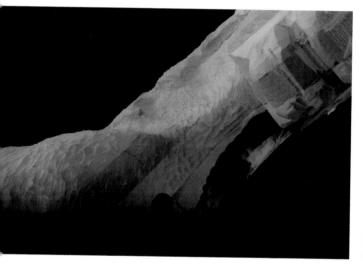

Stay aware of the directions the hair flows. Here on the chest the hair from the two sides converges in sort of a V.

and set the line of the nostril flare a U-gouge.

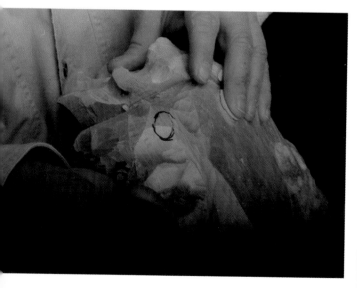
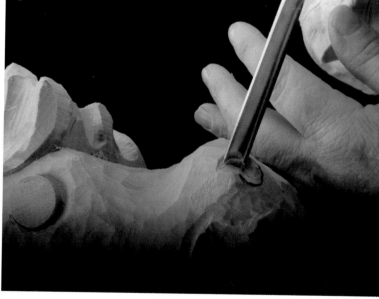

The nose area remains smooth, so you will need to clean it up with gouge.

Open up the nostril flare.

47

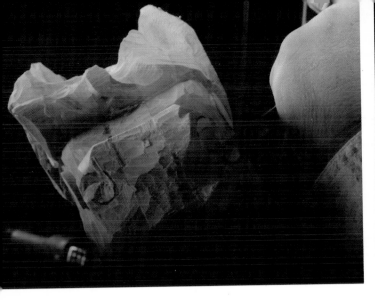

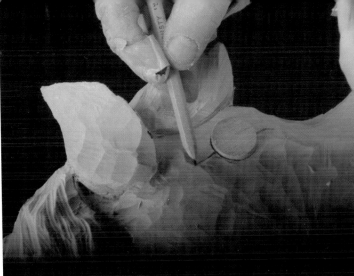

Finally run a channel around the nostril, leaving a ridge of about 1/4" to accentuate the flare.

Draw a line into the eye, about even with the bottom of the ear. On the other side of the eye it comes out at the same level and turns down toward the nose.

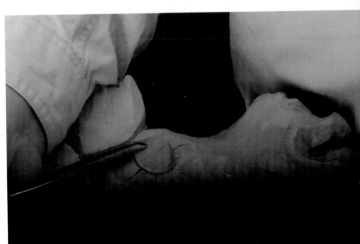

The result.

Begin rounding off the eyeball by knocking off the edge.

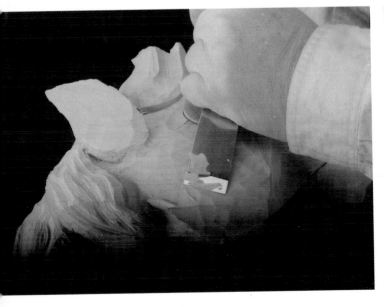

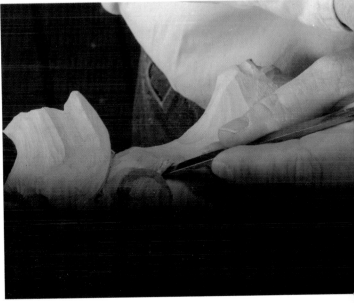

I take off the high points of the cheek with a straight chisel. This will make it much easier to sand.

Cut a triangle at the front of the eye...

and at the back.

A smaller gouge is used to cut shorter channels at the front and back of the top of the eye. This is enough to create the upper lid.

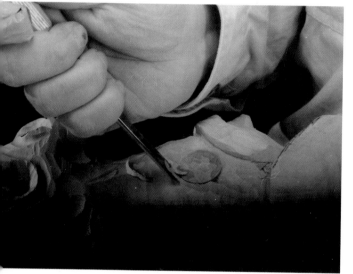

Cut around the pupil to open up the eye.

As I go over details, I need to clean out the inside of the ear a little more.

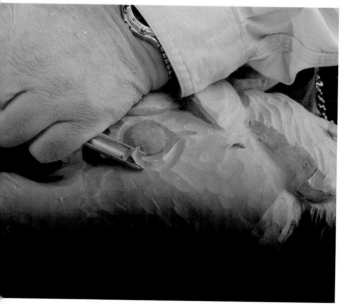

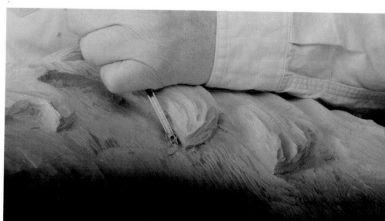

With a gouge, cut a groove below the eye creating a lid.

A veiner will add the hair texture to places that the power tool would not reach. A small burr on the rotary tool would also work. Whichever tool, the result you want should look like the rest of the hair texture and should blend inconspicuously.

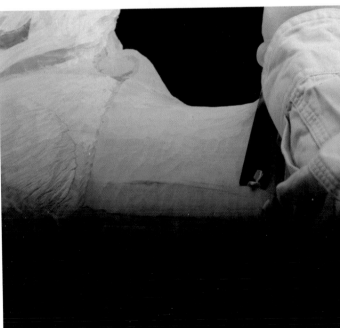

Use a commercial filler to close up the gaps. This is an ash-toned filler, that should come pretty close to the basswood I am using.

The stirrup piece of the saddle is from a piece of basswood about 7 1/2" x 4". It is 1" thick at the bottom and tapers to nothing at the top. Each of these will need to be custom fit to your saddle. The footrest is a length of 1" hardwood dowel, protruding about 3 1/2". The hole in the stirrup piece should be centered about 1 1/2" up from the bottom, and 1 1/2" in from the front.

While the wood putty sets up, I'll smooth the leather. this may be sanded, but I'm going to give it a textured leather look with the short strokes of a chisel.

Glue the stirrup pieces in place and let them set.

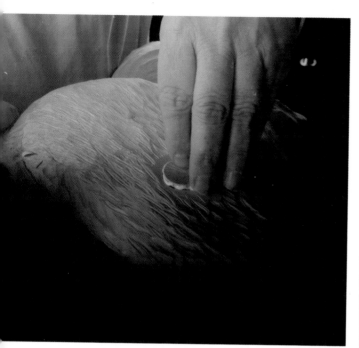

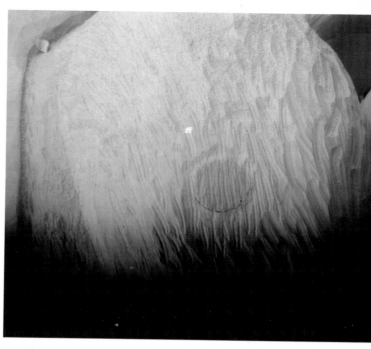

The result.

Glue cross-sections of 1" dowel to plug the bolt holes in the legs.

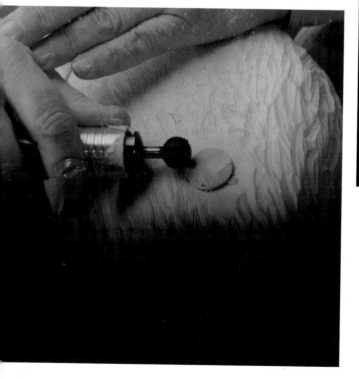

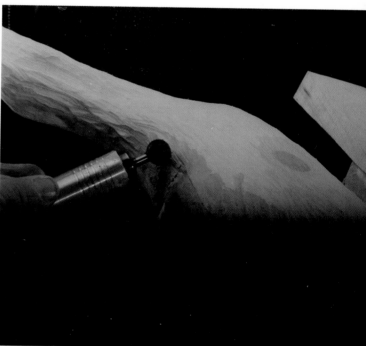

Carve away the excess filler, again blending with the surrounding area.

When the glue has set, carve the plug to blend into the leg.

STAINING THE ROCKING HORSE

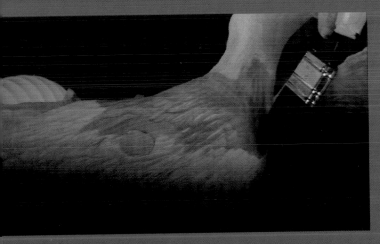

A sealer coat will help the stain go on more evenly.

Add a semi-gloss finish.

Apply a coat of stain to help even out the wood.

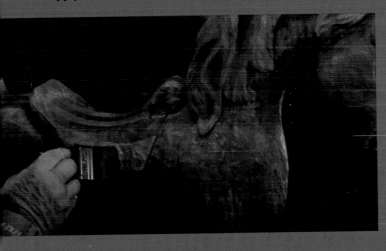

Follow the directions for the stain you are using. In this case it calls for a second coat after the first has dried.

Glue the foot rests in place.

THE GALLERY

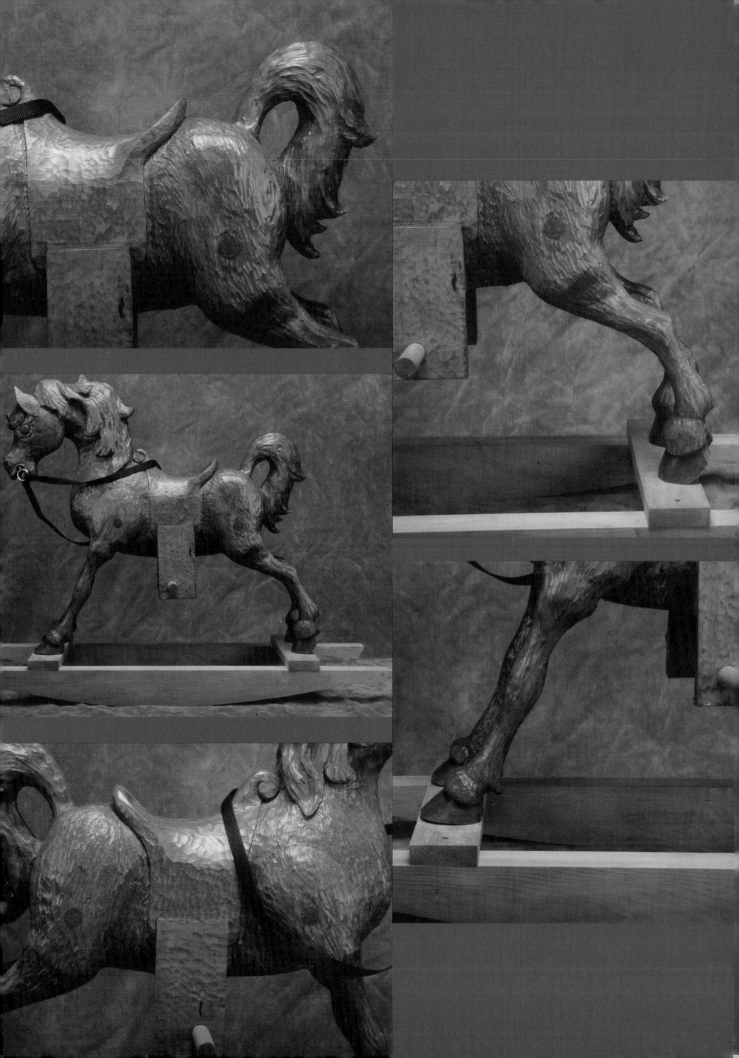

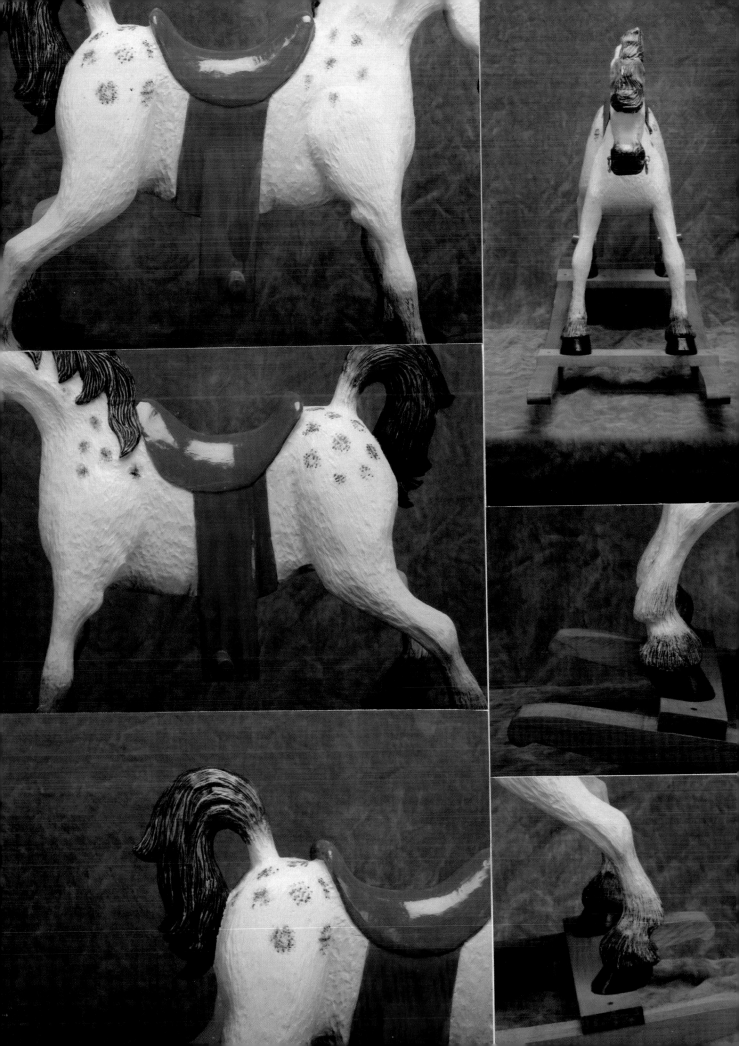

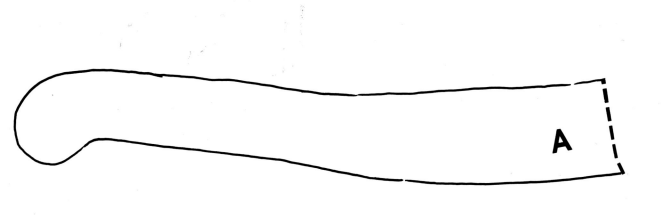

The runners at 1/3 size.

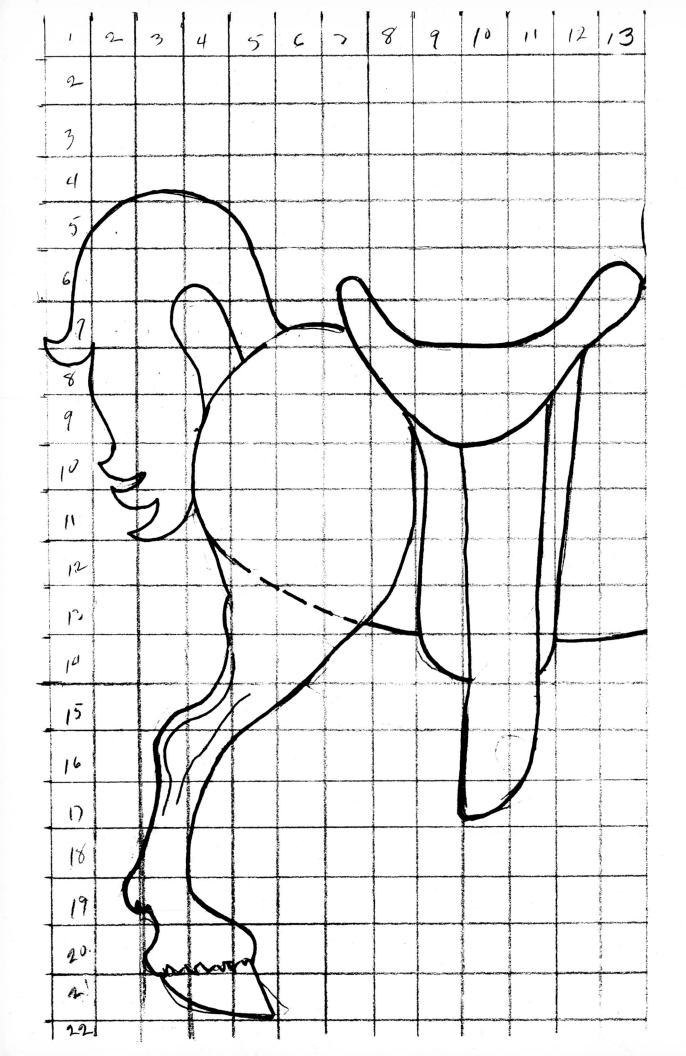

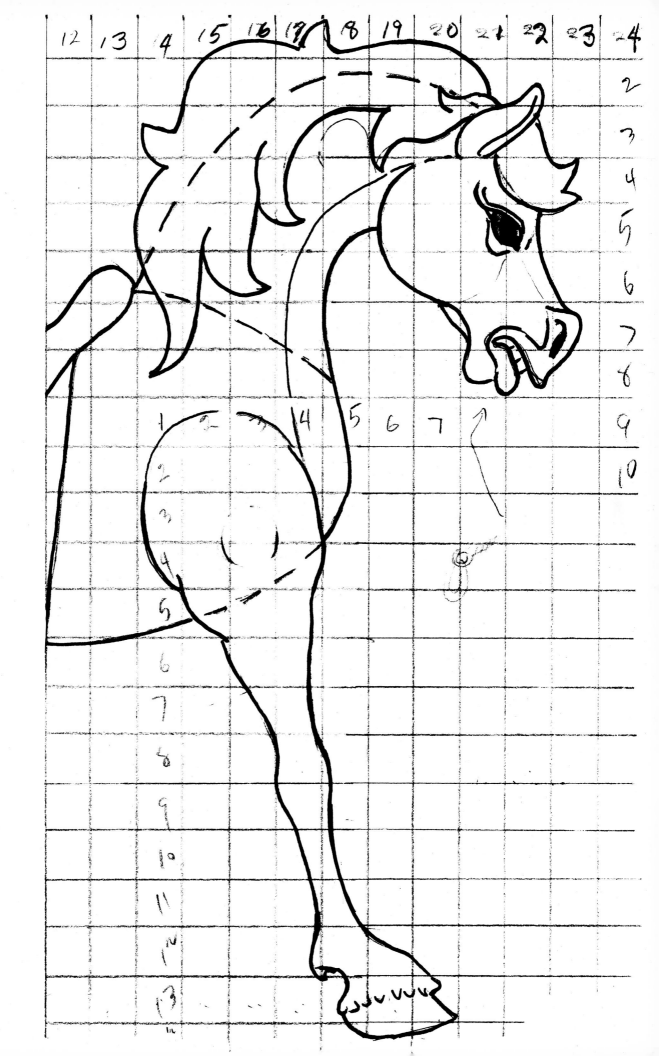

Pattern for a Toy Rocking Horse at 65% of carved size. Enlarge 152% to attain original size, or use at any size you wish.

An overall view of the pattern.

PATTERNS

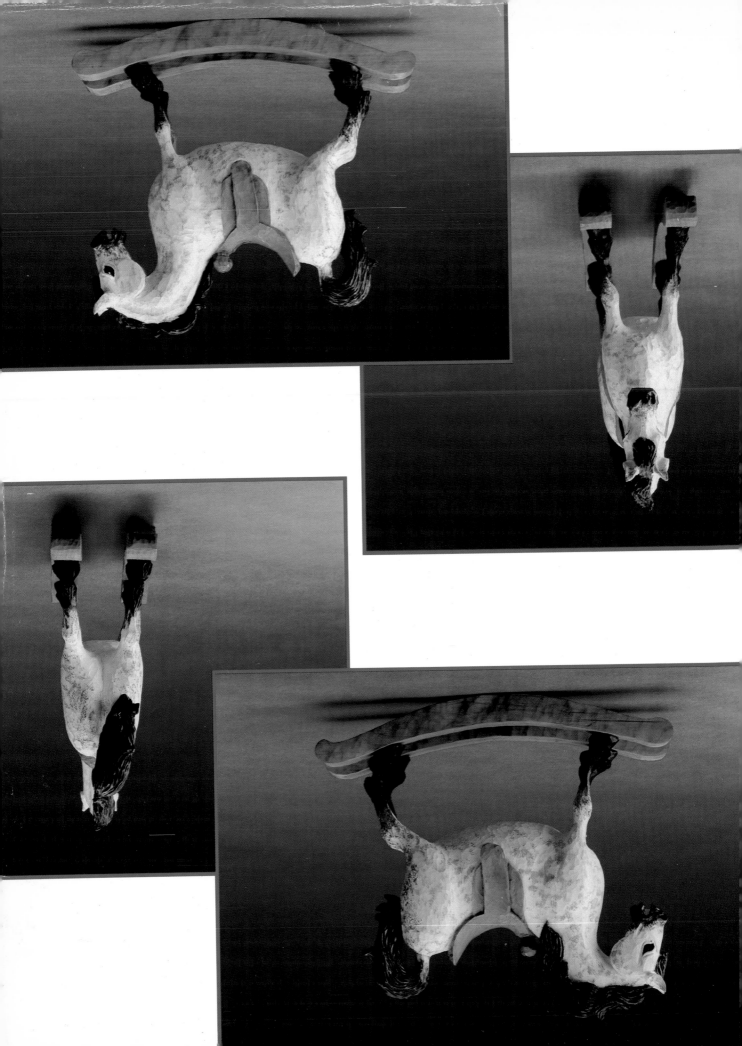